The Campout Cookbook

Homemade Camping Recipes to Make in The Woods

BY

Daniel Humphreys

Copyright 2019 Daniel Humphreys

License Notes

No part of this Book can be reproduced in any form or by any means including print, electronic, scanning or photocopying unless prior permission is granted by the author.

All ideas, suggestions and guidelines mentioned here are written for informative purposes. While the author has taken every possible step to ensure accuracy, all readers are advised to follow information at their own risk. The author cannot be held responsible for personal and/or commercial damages in case of misinterpreting and misunderstanding any part of this Book

Table of Contents

Introduction

The wonderful thing about camping is the fact that it gives you the chance to get away from your hectic life while allowing you to prepare wonderful memories in the process. However, what many people often assume with camping is that you need to eat only prepackaged foods or simple meals. In fact, you can make restaurant quality meals that you can only make over an open fire.

That is what I hope to teach you throughout the pages of this cookbook. By the end of this cookbook, I hope not only that you have learned how to prepare meals over an open flame, but find a few new recipes that will leave you full as you explore nature. With the help of over 25 delicious camping recipes, I hope that this possibility becomes a reality for you.

So, let's stop wasting time and get to cooking!

Skillet Peach Cobbler

This is the perfect skillet dish to make whenever you are craving something sweet while you are out camping.

Makes: 8 servings

Total Prep Time: 1 hour

Ingredients:

- 2 cups of all-purpose flour
- 1 ½ cups of white sugar
- 2 tsp. of baking powder
- 2 tsp. of salt
- 2 eggs, beaten
- 1 ½ cups of crème fraiche, evenly divided
- 1 cup of whole milk
- 2 tsp. of pure vanilla
- ¼ cup of butter, soft
- 2 pounds of peaches, pits removed, peeled and cut into wedges
- 1 cup of peach preserves
- 1 cup of heavy whipping cream
- 2 Tbsp. of white sugar

Directions:

1. Preheat the oven to 350 degrees.

2. In a bowl, add in the all-purpose flour, white sugar, dash of salt and baking powder. Stir well to mix.

3. In a separate bowl, add in the beaten eggs, crème fraiche, whole milk and pure vanilla. Whisk until mixed. Add in the flour mix. Whisk until smooth in consistency.

4. In a skillet set over medium heat, add in the butter. Once melted, remove from heat. Pour in the batter.

5. Sprinkle the peach wedges over the top.

6. Place into the oven to bake for 45 to 50 minutes or until baked through. Remove and set aside to cool slightly.

7. In a bowl, add in the heavy whipping cream. Beat with an electric mixer until peaks begin to form on the surface. Add in the white sugar and 1 cup of crème fraiche. Continue to beat until mixed. Dollop over the top of the cobbler.

8. Serve immediately with the peach peaches.

Camping Breakfast Sandwiches

If you want to try to turn your camping experience into a fancy endeavor, then this is the perfect dish for you to achieve that.

Makes: 4 servings

Total Prep Time: 25 minutes

Ingredients:

- 4 sour dough English muffins
- 2 cups of pulled pork, cooked
- 4 eggs
- 4 slices of cheddar cheese
- Butter, for spreading

Directions:

1. Spread butter onto the inside and outside of the English muffins. In a cast iron skillet set over medium heat, add in the English muffins. Cook for 2 minutes or until lightly toasted. Remove and set aside.

2. In the same skillet, add in pulled pork. Cook for 1 to 2 minutes or until piping hot. Set aside.

3. Crack the eggs in the skillet. Cook for 2 to 3 minutes or until the egg whites are set.

4. Add ¼ cup of the pulled pork onto the English muffin. Top off with the fried eggs and slice of cheddar cheese. Repeat with the remaining English muffins.

5. Wrap the English muffins in sheets of aluminum foil. Set over a campfire. Cook for 1 to 2 minutes or until the cheese melts.

6. Remove and serve immediately.

Classic S'mores

This is a delicious s'mores recipe that you can make along with your children while you are camping to make precious memories.

Makes: 24 servings

Total Prep Time: 30 minutes

Ingredients:

- 1 cup of butter, melted
- 1/3 cup of white sugar
- 3 cups of graham cracker crumbs
- 2 cups of semi-sweet chocolate chips
- 3 cups of miniature marshmallows

Directions:

1. Preheat the oven to 350 degrees. Grease a baking dish with butter.

2. In a bowl, add in the melted butter, white sugar and graham cracker crumbs. Stir well to mix. Spread half of this mix into the bottom of the baking dish.

3. Top off with the semi-sweet chocolate chips and miniature marshmallows. Sprinkle the remaining graham cracker mix over the top. Press down slightly.

4. Place into the oven to bake for 10 minutes or until the marshmallows are melted.

5. Remove and set aside to cool completely.

6. Slice into squares and serve.

Cornmeal Griddle Pancakes

This is the perfect pancake dish to make to kick off your morning whenever you are camping. Serve with a cup of coffee for the tastiest results.

Makes: 4 servings

Total Prep Time: 15 minutes

Ingredients:

- ¾ cup of cornmeal
- 1 ¼ cup of all-purpose flour
- 2 Tbsp. of white sugar
- 1 Tbsp. of baking powder
- 1 tsp. of salt
- 1 1/8 cup of whole milk
- 1 egg
- 1 Tbsp. of butter, melted and cooled

Directions:

1. In a bowl, add in all of the ingredients. Stir well until smooth in consistency.

2. Add a griddle over medium heat, add in 1 tablespoon of butter. Once melted, add in ¼ cup of the pancake mix. Cook for 2 to 3 minutes. Flip and continue to cook for an additional 2 to 3 minutes or until golden.

3. Remove and repeat.

4. Serve immediately.

Dutch Oven Cornbread

This is a delicious cornbread recipe that will fill you up in the morning on the trail. Made with fig jam, this is a breakfast dish I know you will want to make every morning.

Makes: 10 servings

Total Prep Time: 45 minutes

Ingredients:

- ¾ cup of butter
- 1 ½ cups of all-purpose flour
- 1 ½ cups of cornmeal
- ¼ cup of white sugar
- 2 tsp. of baking soda
- 2 tsp. of salt
- ½ tsp. of baking powder
- 3 eggs
- 1 cup of whole milk
- ¾ cup of fig jam

Directions:

1. Preheat the oven to 425 degrees.

2. Grease a Dutch oven with butter. Set over medium heat until melted. Swirl around to coat the bottom and pour the melted butter into a bowl.

3. In a bowl, add in the all-purpose flour, cornmeal, white sugar, dash of salt, baking powder and soda. Stir well to mix. Add in the eggs and whole milk. Whisk until mixed. Pour into the Dutch oven.

4. Cover and set into the oven to bake for 10 to 12 minutes.

5. Dot the top of the cornbread with the fig jam. Cover and continue to bake for an additional 15 to 20 minutes or until baked through.

6. Remove and set aside to cool for 15 minutes before serving.

Cheese Garlic Fries

These are the easiest and cheesiest fries you can ever make. They are much healthier than any other kind of fries that you can make.

Makes: 4 servings

Total Prep Time: 50 minutes

Ingredients:

- 2 Tbsp. of extra virgin olive oil
- 4 cloves of garlic, minced
- ½ tsp. of crushed red pepper flakes
- Dash of salt and black pepper
- 1 pound of red potatoes, cut into wedges
- 1 cup of sharp cheddar cheese, shredded
- 2 Tbsp. of sour cream
- 2 Tbsp. of chives, chopped

Directions:

1. Preheat the oven to 400 degrees. Line a baking sheet with a sheet of aluminum foil.

2. In a bowl, add in the olive oil, minced garlic and crushed red pepper flakes. Season with a dash of salt and black pepper. Whisk well until mixed.

3. Add the potato wedges onto the baking sheet. Fold the sides of the foil around the potatoes. Pour the oil mixture over the top. Seal the foil packet.

4. Place into the oven to bake for 30 to 35 minutes or until the potatoes are soft.

5. Sprinkle the shredded cheddar cheese over the top. Continue to broil for 2 to 3 minutes or until melted.

6. Remove. Serve immediately with a garnish of sour cream and chopped chives.

Camping Breakfast Cookies

These are the most delicious cookies to prepare whenever you are craving something on the sweeter side.

Makes: 24 servings

Total Prep Time: 25 minutes

Ingredients:

- 2 cups of white sugar
- 1 cup of peanut butter
- 1 cup of butter
- ½ cup of water
- 2 Tbsp. of pure vanilla
- 2 eggs
- 2 ¼ cups of all-purpose flour
- 1 tsp. of baking soda
- ½ tsp. of salt
- 1 ½ cups of rolled oats
- 1 ½ cups of raisins
- 6 cups of Cheerios, toasted

Directions:

1. Preheat the oven to 375 degrees.

2. In a bowl, add in the white sugar, peanut butter, butter, water, pure vanilla and eggs. Beat with an electric mixer until smooth in consistency. Add in the all-purpose flour, dash of salt and baking soda. Stir well until mixed.

3. Add in the rolled oats, raisins and Cheerios. Stir well to evenly mixed.

4. Drop ½ cup of the dough onto cookie sheets. Flatten until 1 inch in thickness.

5. Place into the oven to bake for 10 to 12 minutes or until browned around the edges.

6. Remove and cool completely before serving.

Eggs and Corned Beef Hash

This corned beef hash dish is made with a crispy texture and a ton of flavor, I know you will fall in love with it.

Makes: 6 servings

Total Prep Time: 1 hour and 20 minutes

Ingredients for the salsa:

- 6 dried New Mexico chiles, seeds removed and stems removed
- ¼ of a red onion, chopped
- 1 clove of garlic, minced
- 2 Tbsp. of extra virgin olive oil
- 2 Tbsp. of white balsamic vinegar

Ingredients for the hash and eggs:

- 6 Tbsp. of butter
- 1 red onion, thinly sliced
- 6 cloves of garlic, smashed
- 2 cups of green cabbage, thinly sliced
- 1 ½ pounds of Yukon gold potatoes, peeled and grated
- 1 tsp. of four seasons seasoning
- 12 ounces of corned beef, cooked and cut into pieces
- 6 eggs
- ¼ cup of flat leaf parsley, chopped

Directions:

1. Prepare the salsa. In a bowl, add in boiling water. Add in the New Mexico chilies. Cover and set aside to rest for 15 to 20 minutes or until soft. Drain the chiles and reserve the liquid.

2. In a blender, add in the soaked chilies, chopped red onion, minced garlic, olive oil, white vinegar and ¼ cup of the soaked liquid. Blend on the highest setting until smooth in consistency. Pour into a bowl and set aside.

3. Prepare the hash and eggs. In a skillet set over medium to high heat, add in the butter. Once melted, add in the sliced red onions, smashed garlic and sliced green cabbage. Stir well to mix. Cook for 15 to 20 minutes or until crispy around the edges.

4. Add in the grated potatoes and four seasons seasoning. Stir well to mix. Continue to cook for 20 to 25 minutes or until cooked through.

5. Add in the corned beef pieces and fold gently to incorporate. Continue to cook for 5 minutes or until crispy.

6. Use the back of a spoon and create small wells in the surface of the corned beef mix. Crack the eggs into each of the wells.

7. Cover and lower the heat to low. Cook for 8 to 10 minutes or until the egg whites are set.

8. Top off with the chopped parsley and salsa. Serve immediately.

Campfire Skillet Berry Cake

This is a tasty dessert that everybody will love, especially if you have a strong sweet tooth that needs to be satisfied.

Makes: 4 to 6 servings

Total Prep Time: 20 minutes

Ingredients:

- 12 to 16 ounces of berries
- 2 Tbsp. of white sugar
- ¼ cup of butter
- ¾ pound of pound cake
- 2 rolo candy bars

Directions:

1. In a bowl, add in the berries and white sugar. Stir well to mix. Set aside to rest for 10 to 15 minutes.

2. Place a grate over a campfire. Add the skillet over the grate and add in the butter. Allow to melt.

3. Slice the pound cake into small cubes and add into the skillet. Cook for 1 to 2 minutes or until toasted on all sides. Remove the skillet from heat.

4. Sprinkle the berries over the top of the pound cake cubes. Sprinkle the rolo candy bars over the top.

5. Cover with a sheet of aluminum foil. Place back onto the campfire. Allow to cook for 8 to 10 minutes or until the candy bars melt.

6. Remove and serve immediately.

Grilled Peanut Butter Cup Sandwiches

These sandwiches are so delicious, even the pickiest of eaters will be begging for seconds. This will become a camping favorite.

Makes: 2 servings

Total Prep Time: 10 minutes

Ingredients:

- 2 tsp. of margarine
- 2 slices of white bread
- 1 ½ Tbsp. of peanut butter
- 2 Tbsp. of semisweet chocolate chips

Directions:

1. Spread 1 teaspoon of margarine onto one side of the bread slices. Place the butter sides together.

2. Spread the peanut butter onto one slice of the bread slices. Sprinkle the semi-sweet chocolate chips over the top. Top off with the bread slice with the butter side facing out.

3. In a skillet set over medium heat. Add in the sandwich. Grill for 3 to 4 minutes or until gold.

4. Remove and slice in half. Serve immediately.

Soy Sauce and Citrus Chicken

This delicious chicken is marinated in a vinegar and citrus marinade that makes for a sweet tasting dinner I know you will love.

Makes: 4 servings

Total Prep Time: 13 hours

Ingredients for the chicken:

- 4 cloves of garlic, crushed
- 1, 2 inch piece of ginger, crushed
- 1 cup of citrus juice
- ½ cup of soy sauce
- 1/3 cup of distilled white vinegar
- ¼ cup of white sugar
- 1, 4 pound chicken, backbone removed and cut into halves
- Dash of salt

Ingredients for the dipping sauce:

- 1 stalk of lemongrass stalk, sliced
- 2 shallots, cut into halves
- 2 scallions, chopped
- 1 red chile, seeds removed and chopped
- 4 cloves of garlic, unpeeled
- 1, 1 inch piece of ginger, peeled and chopped
- 2 Tbsp. of fish sauce
- 2 Tbsp. of lime juice
- 1 tsp. of white sugar
- Cilantro leaves, chopped

Directions:

1. Prepare the chicken. In a bowl, add in the crushed garlic, crushed ginger, citrus juice, white vinegar and white sugar. Stir well to mix. Pour into a Ziploc bag. Add in the chicken halves and seal the bag. Set into the fridge to marinate for 12 hours.

2. Preheat the oven to 425 degrees.

3. Remove the chicken from the marinade. Pat dry with a few paper towels. Season with a dash of salt. Place onto a baking sheet lined with a sheet of aluminum foil. Place into the oven to roast for 30 to 40 minutes or until cooked through. Remove and set aside.

4. Prepare the dipping sauce. In a saucepan set over medium heat, add in 1 ½ cup of water. Allow to come to a boil. Add in the lemongrass and boil for 8 to 10 minutes or until fragrant. Remove and strain through a sieve into a bowl.

5. In a skillet set over medium to high heat, add in the shallots, chopped scallions, chopped chile and garlic. Cook for 8 to 10 minutes or until browned. Remove from heat and set aside to cool. Chop finely.

6. Transfer into the lemon grass mix. Add in the fish sauce, lime juice and white sugar. Stir well to mix. Set aside.

7. Sieve the infusion through a sieve into a separate bowl.

8. Transfer the roasted chicken onto a serving plate. Pour the dipping sauce over the top.

9. Serve immediately.

Campfire S'mores Granola

This is an easy to make and delicious granola that can be made right in time for your next outdoor getaway.

Makes: 6 servings

Total Prep Time: 20 minutes

Ingredients:

- 3 cups of rolled oats
- ¼ cup of gluten free oat bran
- Dash of powdered cinnamon
- Dash of sea salt
- 1 Tbsp. of butter
- ¼ cup of maple syrup
- 1 cup of miniature marshmallows
- 1 cup of chocolate chips

Directions:

1. Add a sheet of aluminum foil onto a baking sheet. Grease with cooking spray.

2. In a bowl, add in the rolled oats, oat bran, powdered cinnamon and dash of sea salt. Stir well to mix. Add in the butter and maple syrup. Stir well until incorporated.

3. Add a layer of the mix onto the baking sheet.

4. Cover and set over a campfire to cook for 5 to 10 minutes.

5. Remove and set aside to cool completely.

6. In a fire proof bowl, add in the miniature marshmallows and chocolate chips. Cook for 5 minutes or until melted. Drizzle over the top of the granola.

7. Slice into bars and serve.

Fire Roasted Bread

This delicious quick bread is made just for camping. It is a dense bread that is packed full of nutrients, making it one of the healthiest bread dishes you can make today.

Makes: 36 servings

Total Prep Time: 1 hour

Ingredients:

- 1 ½ cups of whole wheat flour
- 1 ½ cups of all-purpose flour
- 1 ¼ cup of rolled oats
- ¾ cup of light brown sugar
- 1 ½ tsp. of baking powder
- 1 tsp. of salt
- 2 eggs
- ½ cup of honey
- ¼ cup of molasses
- 1 cup of applesauce
- ½ cup of vegetable oil
- 1 cup of raisins
- 2/3 cup of sunflower seeds

Directions:

1. Preheat the oven to 350 degrees. Grease two baking dishes.

2. In a bowl, add in the whole wheat flour, all-purpose flour, rolled oats, light brown sugar, dash of salt and baking powder. Stir well to mix.

3. In a separate bowl, add in the eggs, honey, molasses, applesauce and vegetable oil. Stir well to mix. Pour into the flour mix. Stir well until just mixed.

4. Add in the raisins and sunflower seeds. Fold to incorporate.

5. Pour into the baking dishes.

6. Place into the oven to bake for 45 minutes or until baked through.

7. Remove and cool for 10 minutes before serving.

Campfire Cherry Hand Pies

This is another sweet tasting dish you can make whenever you are craving something on the sweeter side.

Makes: 8 servings

Total Prep Time: 10 minutes

Ingredients:

- 1 pack of pre-made pie crusts
- 1, 14 ounce can of cherry pie filling
- ¼ cup of white sugar
- Vegetable oil, for greasing

Directions:

1. Roll out the premade pie crust onto a flat surface. Use the top of a wine glass and cut out circles from the dough that are 2 to 3 inches wide.

2. On half of the circles, add a dollop of the cherry pie filling. Top off with the remaining dough circles. Crimp the edges to seal.

3. In a Dutch oven set over a campfire, add in 2 to 3 inches of vegetable oil. Once shimmering, add in the hand pies. Fry for 5 minutes or until golden.

4. Remove and roll the pies immediately in the white sugar.

5. Repeat with the remaining hand pies.

6. Serve immediately.

Pan Seared Pork Chops

If you are looking for a filling meal to enjoy around the campfire, then this is the perfect dish for you to make.

Makes: 4 servings

Total Prep Time: 20 minutes

Ingredients:

- 2 pounds of pork chops, bone-in
- Dash of salt and black pepper
- 1 tsp. of white sugar, evenly divided
- 2 Tbsp. + ¼ cup of extra virgin olive oil
- 1 lemon, zest only
- 1 clove of garlic, grated
- 1 Tbsp. of Dijon mustard
- 1 tsp. of dried oregano
- ¼ tsp. of powdered cumin
- ½ bunch of cilantro leaves, chopped

Directions:

1. Season the pork chops with a dash of salt and black pepper.

2. In a skillet set over medium to high heat, add in 2 tablespoons of olive oil. Add in the pork chops and cook for 5 minutes on each side or until browned. Remove and set aside to rest for 10 minutes.

3. In a bowl, add in the lemon zest, lemon juice, grated garlic, Dijon mustard, dried oregano, powdered cumin and ½ tsp. of white sugar. Whisk until mixed. Add in ¼ cup of the olive oil and whisk well to emulsify. Add in the chopped cilantro leaves. Fold to incorporate. Season with a dash of salt and black pepper.

4. Pour half of the dressing onto a serving plate. Transfer the pork chops over the top. Pour the rest of the dressing over the top.

5. Serve.

Campfire Breakfast Apple Crisp

This is a sweet and healthy way to start of your breakfast in the woods. It is easy to make and can be ready to eat in just a matter of minutes.

Makes: 2 servings

Total Prep Time: 10 minutes

Ingredients:

- 2 to 3 Tbsp. of coconut oil
- ½ cup of rolled oats
- Dash of salt
- ½ tsp. of powdered cinnamon
- 1 Tbsp. of maple syrup
- 2 tsp. of hemp seeds
- 2 Tbsp. of almonds, chopped
- 2 gala apples, peeled and chopped

Directions:

1. Place a cast iron skillet over a low burning fire.

2. In the skillet, add in the coconut oil. Swirl around until it melts. Add in the rolled oats and toss well to coat. Cook for 2 minutes or until toasted.

3. Add in the dash of salt, powdered cinnamon and maple syrup. Toss well to mix.

4. Add in the hemp seeds and chopped almonds over the top.

5. Add the chopped apples and toss to mix. Cook for 5 minutes or until crispy.

6. Remove and serve immediately.

Camping No Bake Cookies

There is no other cookie recipe that is as easy to make as this particular cookie dish. Since you don't have to worry about baking these cookies, you don't have to worry about starting a fire to bake these cookies.

Makes: 18 servings

Total Prep Time: 10 minutes

Ingredients:

- ½ cup of butter, soft
- 2/3 cup of white sugar
- 3 Tbsp. of unsweetened powdered cocoa
- 1 Tbsp. of brewed coffee
- ½ tsp. of pure vanilla
- 1 ¾ cups of rolled oats
- 1/3 cup of powdered sugar, for dusting

Directions:

1. In a bowl, add in the butter, white sugar, powdered cocoa, brewed coffee and pure vanilla. Whisk well to mix until creamy in consistency.

2. Add in the rolled oats. Stir well to incorporate.

3. Divide the mix into 36, 1 inch balls.

4. Roll the cookie balls in the powdered sugar. Place onto a baking sheet lined with a sheet of parchment paper.

5. Serve.

Campfire Nachos

This is a popular campfire dish that all of your camping neighbors will be begging you for the recipe. It is so delicious, I guarantee you will want to make it every camping trip.

Makes: 2 servings

Total Prep Time: 15 minutes

Ingredients:

- 1 Tbsp. of canola oil
- ½ pound of tortilla chips
- 1, 7.75 ounce can of hot tomato sauce
- 1 cup of Mexican cheese blend, shredded
- 1, 14.5 ounce can of black beans, drained
- 1 avocado, cut into cubes
- 4 to 5 green onions, thinly sliced
- 1 handful of cilantro, chopped
- 1 lime, cut into wedges

Directions:

1. In a Dutch oven, add in the canola oil. Swirl around to coat the bottom.

2. Add a layer of 1/3 of the tortilla chips followed can ¼ of the hot tomato sauce, ¼ of the can of black beans, ¼ of the shredded Mexican cheese, 1 handful of avocado cubes, a layer of sliced green onions and a layer of chopped cilantro. Repeat these layers once more.

3. For the third layer, add the remaining tortilla chips, remaining hot tomato sauce, remaining black beans, remaining shredded cheese, chopped avocado, chopped onions and chopped cilantro.

4. Cover and set the Dutch oven over a campfire. Cook for 10 minutes or until the cheese melts.

5. Serve immediately with a garnish of lime wedges.

Campfire Chicken Pot Pie

If you love the taste of chicken pot pie, then this is definitely one dish you are going to want to make every time you go camping.

Makes: 6 servings

Total Prep Time: 55 minutes

Ingredients:

- 2, 29 ounce cans of mixed vegetables with potatoes
- 1, 10.75 ounce can of cream of chicken soup
- 1, 10.75 ounce can of cream of mushroom soup
- 2 chicken breasts, cooked and cut into cubes
- 1, 10 ounce can of biscuit dough

Directions:

1. In a Dutch oven set over preheated campfire coals, add in the cans of mixed vegetables, cream of chicken soup, cream of mushroom soup and chicken cubes. Stir well to mix. Cook for 15 minutes or until hot.

2. Add the biscuit dough in segments over the top of the soup mix.

3. Cover and cook for 15 to 30 minutes or until the biscuits are gold.

4. Remove and serve immediately.

Dutch Oven Mountain Breakfast

This is the filling campfire dish you can make whenever you are spending a night of the mountain. It is filling and will give your body the energy it needs to keep on hiking.

Makes: 12 servings

Total Prep Time: 1 hour and 30 minutes

Ingredients:

- 1 pound of mild pork sausage
- 1 onion, chopped
- 1 clove of garlic, minced
- 1 red bell pepper, chopped
- 1 green bell pepper, chopped
- 1, 2pound pack of hash brown potatoes, shredded
- 12 eggs, beaten
- 1, 16 ounce pack of cheddar cheese, shredded

Directions:

1. Preheat a campfire with a bed of coals.

2. In a Dutch set over the coals, add in the mild pork sausage, chopped onion and minced garlic. Cover and cook for 8 to 10 minutes or until the sausage is cooked through.

3. Add in the chopped red bell pepper, chopped green bell pepper and shredded hash brown potatoes. Cook for 15 minutes or until soft.

4. Pour in the beaten eggs. Cover and continue to cook for an additional 40 minutes or until the eggs are firm.

5. Sprinkle the shredded cheddar cheese over the top. Continue to cook for 5 minutes or until melted.

6. Remove and serve immediately.

Miniature Quiche

This is a delicious camping dish you can make for those picky eaters in your home. It makes for the perfect snack to enjoy after a long hike in the woods.

Makes: 12 servings

Total Prep Time: 30 minutes

Ingredients:

- 3 eggs
- 1 ½ cup of swiss cheese, shredded
- 1 pack of creamy spinach
- 2 Tbsp. of bacon bits
- ½ cup of ham, cut into cubes
- ¾ cup of mushrooms, thinly sliced
- 2 premade pie crusts

Directions:

1. Unroll the pie crusts onto a flat surface. Use the top part of a glass and cut out 3 to 4 inch circles from the dough. Place into a greased muffin pan in the individual muffin cups.

2. In a bowl, add in the shredded cheese, eggs, bacon bits, sliced mushrooms and creamy spinach. Stir well to mix.

3. Pour the egg mix into the muffin cups.

4. Top off with extra dough circles and cut slits in the top for venting.

5. Place into the oven to bae for 15 minutes at 275 degrees or until browned around the edges.

6. Remove and cool for 10 minutes before serving.

Fire Scalloped Potatoes

If you need to take in your daily dose of carbs while you are camping, then this is the perfect campfire dish for you to prepare.

Makes: 8 servings

Total Prep Time: 45 minutes

Ingredients:

- 8 Russet potatoes, peeled and chopped
- 1 bunch of green onions, thinly sliced
- 1, 10 ounce can of cream of mushroom soup, condensed
- 1 cup of cheddar cheese, shredded
- Dash of black pepper
- Dash of garlic salt
- ½ cup of bacon, cooked and crumbled
- ½ cup of cooked mushrooms
- ½ cup of butter

Directions:

1. Preheat an outdoor grill to medium heat.

2. Grease 8 sheets of aluminum foil with cooking spray.

3. In a bowl, add in the chopped russet potatoes, sliced green onions, cream of mushroom soup and shredded cheddar cheese. Season with a dash of salt and black pepper. Pour over the sheets of aluminum foil.

4. Dot the top of the mix with butter.

5. Fold the foil over the filling and seal the edges well.

6. Place the foil packets onto the grill. Cook for 15 to 20 minutes or until the potatoes are cooked through.

7. Remove and serve immediately.

Campfire French Toast

This is another delicious breakfast dish that is so easy to make, it will become a camping staple for you and your family.

Makes: 6 servings

Total Prep Time: 45 minutes

Ingredients:

- 1 loaf of French bread
- 8 eggs
- ¼ cup of whole milk
- 1 tsp. of pure vanilla
- 1 tsp. of powdered cinnamon
- ¼ cup of almonds, thinly sliced
- 1 cup of strawberries, thinly sliced
- Powdered sugar, for dusting
- Maple syrup, for serving

Directions:

1. Place the loaf of French bread into a sheet of aluminum foil.

2. Sprinkle the chopped strawberries over the top of the bread loaf followed by the slices almonds.

3. In a bowl, add in the eggs, whole milk, pure vanilla and powdered cinnamon. Whisk until frothy. Pour over the bread and wrap the bread tightly in the aluminum foil.

4. Place over a campfire. Cook for 40 minutes.

5. Remove and allow to rest for 10 minutes.

6. Serve with a dusting of powdered sugar and maple syrup.

Grilled Sausage and Potatoes

This is a filling and delicious campfire dish you can make any time you decide to go camping. It is incredibly easy to make and very satisfying.

Makes: 4 servings

Total Prep Time: 45 minutes

Ingredients:

- ¾ pound of green beans, cut into halves
- ½ pound of red potatoes, cut into quarters
- 1 onion, thinly sliced
- 1 pound of smoked sausage, cut into pieces
- Dash of salt and black pepper
- 1 tsp. of vegetable oil
- 1 tsp. of butter
- 1/3 cup of water

Directions:

1. Preheat an outdoor grill to high heat.

2. On a sheet of aluminum foil, add the green beans halves, red potato quarters, sliced onion and smoked sausage pieces. Season with a dash of salt and black pepper. Dot with butter over the top.

3. Fold the foil over the filling.

4. In a small opening, add in the water. Seal the packets.

5. Place onto the grill. Cover and cook for 20 to 30 minutes or until the vegetables are soft.

6. Remove and serve.

Outdoor Cowboy Casserole

This is a casserole dish that is made with the perfect combination of bacon and hamburger over homemade biscuits, making a dish that will become quickly addicting.

Makes: 5 servings

Total Prep Time: 25 minutes

Ingredients:

- ½ pound of bacon, chopped into small pieces
- 1 pound of lean ground beef
- 1 onion, chopped
- 2, 15 ounce cans of pork baked beans
- 1/3 cup of barbecue sauce
- 1, 7.5 ounce pack of biscuit dough

Directions:

1. In a Dutch oven set over medium heat, add in the bacon. Cook for 5 minutes or until crispy. Remove and set onto a plate lined with paper towels to drain.

2. Add the ground beef and chopped onion into the skillet. Cook for 8 to 10 minutes or until browned. Drain the excess grease.

3. Add in the cooked bacon, baked beans and barbecue. Stir well to mix. Allow to come to a boil. Lower the heat to low.

4. Add in the biscuit dough over the top. Cover and continue to cook for 10 minutes or until the biscuits are cooked through.

5. Remove and serve immediately.

Conclusion

Well, there you have it!

Hopefully by the end of this campfire cookbook, you have found plenty of recipes you can prepare while you are camping. By the end of this cookbook, not only do I hope you have found plenty of new dishes you can make for the whole family while you are roughing out, but feel encouraged that you can eat well while you are camping.

So, what is next for you?

The next step for you to take is to begin making all of these delicious camping recipes for yourself. Once you have done that, take what you have learned inside of this cookbook and make even more delicious camping recipes.

Good luck!

Author's Afterthoughts

Thanks ever so much to each of my cherished readers for investing the time to read this book!

I know you could have picked from many other books but you chose this one. So a big thanks for downloading this book and reading all the way to the end.

If you enjoyed this book or received value from it, I'd like to ask you for a favor. Please take a few minutes to post an honest and heartfelt review on Amazon.com. Your support does make a difference and helps to benefit other people.

Thanks!

Daniel Humphreys

About the Author

Daniel Humphreys

Many people will ask me if I am German or Norman, and my answer is that I am 100% unique! Joking aside, I owe my cooking influence mainly to my mother who was British! I can certainly make a mean Sheppard's pie, but when it comes to preparing Bratwurst sausages and drinking beer with friends, I am also all in!

I am taking you on this culinary journey with me and hope you can appreciate my diversified background. In my 15 years career as a chef, I never had a dish returned to me by one of clients, so that should say something about me!

Actually, I will take that back. My worst critic is my four years old son, who refuses to taste anything that is green color. That shall pass, I am sure.

My hope is to help my children discover the joy of cooking and sharing their creations with their loved ones, like I did all my life. When you develop a passion for cooking and my suspicious is that you have one as well, it usually sticks for life. The best advice I can give anyone as a professional chef is invest. Invest your time, your heart in each meal you are creating. Invest also a little money in good cooking hardware and quality ingredients. But most of all enjoy every meal you prepare with YOUR friends and family!

Manufactured by Amazon.ca
Bolton, ON

36382019R00049